GW00391508

A CENTURY *of*
SUTTON

High Street, looking north from railway station, *c.* 1916. How indicative of the old way of life is the style and variety of trade-names and signs on the shops. Bowling the ironmongers occupied the corner site till relocated to Grove Road in 1926, after which Midland Bank took over the premises. The tea-shop advertised is Riddingtons, which employed my mother and both her parents at different times. Beyond that sign is another, advertising a hair-dressing salon, one of a number of commercial and educational 'upstairs' enterprises.

A CENTURY *of* SUTTON

PATRICIA BERRY

SUTTON PUBLISHING

First published in the United Kingdom in 2000 by Sutton Publishing Limited

This new paperback edition first published in 2007 by
Sutton Publishing, an imprint of NPI Media Group
Cirencester Road · Chalford · Stroud · Gloucestershire · GL6 8PE

Copyright © Patricia Berry, 2000, 2007
Copyright © 'Britain: A Century of Change', Roger Hudson, 2000, 2007

All rights reserved. No part of this publication may be reproduced, stored in a retrieval system, or transmitted, in any form or by any means, electronic, mechanical, photocopying, recording or otherwise, without the prior permission of the publisher and copyright holder.

The author has asserted the moral right to be identified as the author of this work.

British Library Cataloguing in Publication Data
A catalogue record for this book is available from the British Library.

ISBN 978-0-7509-4902-6

Illustrations

Front endpaper: Lower High Street, Sutton, *c.* 1904.
Back endpaper: Nonsuch Mansion, Cheam, 1960s.
Half title page: Belmont Wolf Cubs on parade, 1960s.
Title page: Picnic in Overton's field, Belmont, 1924.

Typeset in Photina.
Typesetting and origination by
Sutton Publishing.
Printed and bound in England.

Bus number 180 at London General Omnibus Company's
Belmont terminus, *c.* 1929.

Contents

West side of High Street, looking towards London, c. 1916. The Station Hotel (extreme left), altered and expanded out of all recognition in the 1970s, may have originated with the coming of the London, Brighton & South Coast Railway to Sutton in 1847. All the shops down to Grove Road remained unaltered until 1932, when the lower four (including Wootton Brothers page 41), which had stood for fifty years, were demolished. Mitre House was built for the International Stores on the site. On the far corner of Grove Road (in the sunlight) was No. 17 High Street, Chandlers Stores, later occupied by the National Provincial Bank.

Britain: A Century
of Change

Two women encumbered with gas masks go about their daily tasks during
the early days of the war. (*Hulton Getty Picture Collection*)

The sixty years ending in 1900 were a period of huge transformation for Britain. Railway stations, post-and-telegraph offices, police and fire stations, gasworks and gasometers, new livestock markets and covered markets, schools, churches, football grounds, hospitals and asylums, water pumping stations and sewerage plants totally altered the urban scene, and the country's population tripled with more than seven out of ten people being born in or moving to the towns. The century that followed, leading up to the Millennium's end in 2000, was to be a period of even greater change.

When Queen Victoria died in 1901, she was measured for her coffin by her grandson Kaiser Wilhelm, the London prostitutes put on black mourning and the blinds came down in the villas and terraces spreading out from the old town centres. These centres were reachable by train and tram, by the new bicycles and still newer motor cars, were connected by the new telephone, and lit by gas or even electricity. The shops may have been full of British-made cotton and woollen clothing but the grocers and butchers were selling cheap Danish bacon, Argentinian beef, Australasian mutton and tinned or dried fish and fruit from Canada, California and South Africa. Most of these goods were carried in British-built-and-crewed ships burning Welsh steam coal.

A the first decade moved on, the Open Spaces Act meant more parks, bowling greens and cricket pitches. The First World War transformed the place of women, as they took over many men's jobs. Its other legacies were the war memorials which joined the statues of Victorian worthies in main squares round the land. After 1918 death duties and higher taxation bit hard, and a quarter of England changed hands in the space of only a few years.

The multiple shop – the chain store – appeared in the high street: Sainsburys, Maypole, Lipton's, Home & Colonial, the Fifty Shilling Tailor, Burton, Boots, W.H. Smith. The shopper was spoilt for choice, attracted by the brash fascias and advertising hoardings for national brands like Bovril, Pears Soap, and Ovaltine. Many new buildings began to be seen, such as garages, motor showrooms, picture palaces (cinemas), 'palais de dance', and ribbons of 'semis' stretched along the roads and new bypasses and onto the new estates nudging the green belts.

During the 1920s cars became more reliable and sophisticated as well as commonplace, with developments like the electric self-starter making them easier for women to drive. Who wanted to turn a crank handle in the new short skirt? This was, indeed, the electric age as much as the motor era. Trolley buses, electric trams and trains extended mass transport and electric light replaced gas in the street and the home, which itself was groomed by the vacuum cleaner.

A major jolt to the march onward and upward was administered by the Great Depression of the early 1930s. The older British industries

– textiles, shipbuilding, iron, steel, coal – were already under pressure from foreign competition when this worldwide slump arrived. Luckily there were new diversions to alleviate the misery. The 'talkies' arrived in the cinemas; more and more radios and gramophones were to be found in people's homes; there were new women's magazines, with fashion, cookery tips and problem pages; football pools; the flying feats of women pilots like Amy Johnson; the Loch Ness Monster; cheap chocolate and the drama of Edward VIII's abdication.

Things were looking up again by 1936 and new light industry was booming in the Home Counties as factories struggled to keep up with the demand for radios, radiograms, cars and electronic goods, including the first television sets. The threat from Hitler's Germany meant rearmament, particularly of the airforce, which stimulated aircraft and aero engine firms. If you were lucky and lived in the south, there was good money to be earned. A semi-detached house cost £450, a Morris Cowley £150. People may have smoked like chimneys but life expectancy, since 1918, was up by 15 years while the birth rate had almost halved.

In some ways it is the little memories that seem to linger longest from the Second World War: the kerbs painted white to show up

A W.H.Smith shop front in Beaconsfield, 1922.

in the blackout, the rattle of ack-ack shrapnel on roof tiles, sparrows killed by bomb blast. The biggest damage, apart from London, was in the south-west (Plymouth, Bristol) and the Midlands (Coventry, Birmingham). Postwar reconstruction was rooted in the Beveridge Report which set out the expectations for the Welfare State. This, together with the nationalisation of the Bank of England, coal, gas, electricity and the railways, formed the programme of the Labour government in 1945.

Times were hard in the late 1940s, with rationing even more stringent than during the war. Yet this was, as has been said, 'an innocent and well-behaved era'. The first let-up came in 1951 with the Festival of Britain and there was another fillip in 1953 from the Coronation, which incidentally gave a huge boost to the spread of TV. By 1954 leisure motoring had been resumed but the Comet – Britain's best hope for taking on the American aviation industry – suffered a series of mysterious crashes. The Suez debacle of 1956 was followed by an acceleration in the withdrawal from Empire, which had begun in 1947 with the Independence of India. Consumerism was truly born with the advent of commercial TV and most homes soon boasted washing machines, fridges, electric irons and fires.

The *Lady Chatterley* obscenity trial in 1960 was something of a straw in the wind for what was to follow in that decade. A collective loss of inhibition seemed to sweep the land, as the Beatles and the Rolling Stones transformed popular music, and retailing, cinema and the theatre were revolutionised. Designers, hairdressers, photographers and models moved into places vacated by an Establishment put to flight by the new breed of satirists spawned by *Beyond the Fringe* and *Private Eye*.

In the 1970s Britain seems to have suffered a prolonged hangover after the excesses of the previous decade. Ulster, inflation and union troubles were not made up for by entry into the EEC, North Sea Oil, Women's Lib or, indeed, Punk Rock. Mrs

Children collecting aluminium to help the war effort, London, 1940s. (*IWM*)

A street party to celebrate the Queen's Coronation, June 1953. (*Hulton Getty Picture Collection*)

Thatcher applied the corrective in the 1980s, as the country moved more and more from its old manufacturing base over to providing services, consulting, advertising, and expertise in the 'invisible' market of high finance or in IT.

The post-1945 townscape has seen changes to match those in the worlds of work, entertainment and politics. In 1952 the Clean Air Act served notice on smogs and pea-souper fogs, smuts and blackened buildings, forcing people to stop burning coal and go over to smokeless sources of heat and energy. In the same decade some of the best urban building took place in the 'new towns' like Basildon, Crawley, Stevenage and Harlow. Elsewhere open warfare was declared on slums and what was labelled inadequate, cramped, back-to-back, two-up, two-down, housing. The new 'machine for living in' was a flat in a high-rise block. The architects and planners who promoted these were in league with the traffic engineers, determined to keep the motor car moving whatever the price in multi-storey car parks, meters, traffic wardens and ring roads. The old pollutant, coal smoke, was replaced by petrol and diesel exhaust, and traffic noise.

Fast food was no longer only a pork pie in a pub or fish-and-chips. There were Indian curry houses, Chinese take-aways and American-style hamburgers, while the drinker could get away from beer in a wine bar. Under the impact of television the big Gaumonts and Odeons closed or were rebuilt as multi-screen cinemas, while the palais de dance gave way to discos and clubs.

Punk rockers demonstrate their anarchic style during the 1970s. (*Barnaby's Picture Library*)

From the late 1960s the introduction of listed buildings and conservation areas, together with the growth of preservation societies, put a brake on 'comprehensive redevelopment'. The end of the century and the start of the Third Millennium see new challenges to the health of towns and the wellbeing of the nine out of ten people who now live urban lives. The fight is on to prevent town centres from dying, as patterns of housing and shopping change, and edge-of-town supermarkets exercise the attractions of one-stop shopping. But as banks and department stores close, following the haberdashers, greengrocers, butchers and ironmongers, there are signs of new growth such as farmers' markets, and corner stores acting as pick-up points where customers collect shopping ordered on-line from web sites.

Millennium celebrations over the Thames
at Westminster, New Year's Eve, 1999.
(*Barnaby's Picture Library*)

Futurologists tell us that we are in stage two of the consumer revolution: a shift from mass consumption to mass customisation driven by a desire to have things that fit us and our particular lifestyle exactly, and for better service. This must offer hope for small city-centre shop premises, as must the continued attraction of physical shopping, browsing and being part of a crowd: in a word, 'shoppertainment'. Another hopeful trend for towns is the growth in the number of young people postponing marriage and looking to live independently, alone, where there is a buzz, in 'swinging single cities'. Theirs is a 'flats-and-cafés' lifestyle, in contrast to the 'family suburbs', and certainly fits in with government's aim of building 60 per cent of the huge amount of new housing needed on 'brown' sites, recycled urban land. There looks to be plenty of life in the British town yet.

Sutton: An Introduction

At the last count (mid-1998) the population of this London borough stood at 177,084; its boundaries extend to Worcester Park on the west, Beddington on the east, north to St Helier and south towards Woodmansterne. A century ago, there were some 27,000 inhabitants of Sutton and Cheam, though the latter at that time was administered by Epsom Rural Council and was not united with Sutton until 1928. Six years later the two, together with parts of North Cheam, Worcester Park and Belmont, formed what was for the next thirty years Sutton Urban District Council. Doubling in size by taking in Carshalton, Wallington and Beddington, today's borough is a powerful Guernsey-shaped area containing the wide range of trades and industries, buildings and open spaces, ages and nationalities that one might now expect.

At its heart, Sutton itself with its pedestrianised area, ring roads and tower blocks, may give the impression of a thoroughly modern town; I hope that this book will demonstrate how it has grown out of the close-knit community of a century ago, and where to look for reminders of that time. Then, it was a small town with modest shops lining the High Street (Brighton Road) and tree-lined avenues of detached houses rising on all sides, many occupied by city businessmen – the pioneer commuters – and their families, and other gentry. Terraces of smaller houses accommodated the local workforce and their families, with employment for men to be had as craftsmen, labourers, farm workers, carters, gardeners, delivery men, shop assistants and the like, with places for some as clerks, teachers and traders. Women (still more than quarter of a century away from full suffrage) were expected to home-make, though more were finding work in schools, shops and offices.

Imagine the sounds, smells and sights of the little town. Traffic consisted of horses and carts (the clop of hooves, the jingle of harness, the rumble of wheels), bicycles (the swish of tyres) and pedestrians, who might well have been the noisiest, for most people had their boots shod with metal 'Blakies' or other protective studs. Opposite West Street, the musical strokes of hammer on anvil might have rung out from Mr Pearson's smithy. There was birdsong from the many trees and gardens and from the mint and lavender fields only a few streets away – and what sweet scents they gave off! The air was diesel-free (though horse-traffic left a sharp tang of dung) but other fumes came from a few manufactories and breweries. The gasworks in Crown Road was without competition for domestic heating and lighting supplies till 1902 when electricity became generally available.

Before the advent of the first picture-houses, people relied for amusement on travelling shows, funfairs and circuses (which often set up on the Green), or they attended football matches (men-only affairs if early photographs are to be believed), or firework displays. With the factory of world-renowned Crystal Palace pyrotechnicians C.T. Brock newly established on Sutton Common, they could be sure of the biggest and best show-pieces. A free entertainment was watching the passing crowds en route to Brighton or the countryside in between. Derby Day was best, with traffic jams of horse-drawn carriages where four roads met at the Cock Hotel, on the way to Epsom racecourse. At Christmas time there were the fantastic street decorations to be viewed, and friendly arguments about which were the best.

My mother (now in her ninety-sixth year) remembers Sutton not much more sophisticated by, say, 1910, than the town a decade earlier as I have described it. Some motor cars essayed the same hill that had daunted those cart-horses, and indeed the Prince Regent's coachman and horses a hundred years before that. Shops now had a wider range of goods, fashions in dress had changed, and Mr Ernest Shinner continued changing the face of the High Street by extending his original (1899) draper's shop till it would one day occupy the whole frontage from Hill Road to St Nicholas Road.

When war came in 1914, the town's young men disappeared from the streets as the army claimed them, but before long a new population of soldiers arrived, to set up training camps in surrounding fields, or to recuperate in local hospitals: the 'blue boys'. Belgian troops marching past Mother's school threw coins into the playground for the children: enemy prisoners spat on local women who one hot day offered them cups of water: 'they had been told we would try to poison them'.

There were warnings of air raids and Zeppelins flew overhead: Mother looked up and saw one through a glass roof where she had mistakenly taken shelter. There were food shortages: on the days when rumours reached Belmont that supplies had arrived at the Maypole grocers in Sutton High Street, a twelve-year-old girl would be sent there on foot before lessons. Uphill all the way back, at the end of her three-mile trek she could hear the school bell ringing . . . A world-wide epidemic of influenza broke out (it came again the next winter) and there was hardly a family anywhere that did not suffer. Then at last came Armistice Day, and she wrote to her soldier father: 'We went down to Sutton to see the sights, all the soldiers were rolling about and singing. Everyone was wearing red white and blue ribbon and the children were carrying small flags. Our men from the war hospital were marching round and playing the band, waving the Allies' flags. I have just heard the church bells ringing, the first for a long time. There won't be any fireworks on account of the rain, but the children have been promised they can stay up and see them when we have them. I am better from the 'flu, it was horrid and some children were much worse than me.'

That family was lucky, for the father came home, even though he carried the scars of trench foot, a skin condition resulting from standing many hours knee deep in mud and rainwater. Others who survived were shell-shocked, blinded, crippled or paralysed; in every town there was mourning for men killed or missing. Funds were raised so that memorials could be erected both to honour those casualties and to caution the world never to let such a disaster recur; Old Comrades groups were formed, many of them superseded by the newly created British Legion, and Poppy Day was instituted.

The twenties and thirties saw such major changes in modes of transport, in the speed and popularity of motor vehicles, that road-widening, realignment of pavements, introduction of traffic signals and many other adjustments had to be made. Cheam village lost its brewery, two public houses (though one was rebuilt), Cheam Court farmhouse, the old bakery opposite the Parochial Rooms and the manor house itself. Several smaller old buildings were also lost in the name of progress, but a number dating from Tudor times were spared, and residents to this day must be grateful to inspired planners and historians who stopped the rot. Other towns in the borough had similar experiences; enemy bombing in the Second World War did some of the demolition work already envisaged, but also destroyed or severely damaged historic buildings we would have preferred to keep. Pressures of modern life have brought great changes to every aspect of our surroundings and, while we may mourn the loss of favourite, familiar buildings and features, we can still recall people and events associated with them.

Sutton Green. In 1905 a visitor wrote about 'the lovely old elms' edging The Green. It remained a semi-rural spot for many years with its aged farmhouse and Mr Skinner's dairy farm nearby at Hall Mead. The Sutton Gas Company's gasometer arose to dominate the view south, trolleybuses had a turn-round point on the Bushey Road corner from 1935, and at the outbreak of war an underground public air-raid shelter was made near the northern end.

15

The addition thirty-five years ago of the boroughs to the east of Sutton, making up today's London borough, had introduced a number of precious historic sites. These included Carew House, with its directly Tudor connections, and parts of the original Croydon aerodrome where early fliers included the late King George VI who, when Duke of York in the Royal Air Force, won his wings there. Eight years on, American Colonel Charles Lindbergh landed his *Spirit of St Louis* there, after his record-breaking solo flight from New York to Paris in 33½ hours. His arrival was witnessed by my newly-married parents, along with 120,000 others. Across the eastern boroughs flows the River Wandle, with its reminders of old milling days, and so back to the lavender fields of fragrant memory.

Sutton High Street, *c.* 1920. William Pile's (stationers) and SMET (electricity and tramcars) well to the fore.

For well over a quarter of the time-span of this book, Sutton and district has been a London borough, a fact that my grandparents – even my parents – would find incredible. The loss, through post-war random demolition, of buildings they had known and loved was curbed to some extent in the 1960s by the growth of conservation societies supported by new regulations, but it was too late to save some significant landmarks. After a long absence, I returned to Sutton on the very day the destruction of Shinners store began and for a moment it seemed that my entire past was being wiped out with it; now I see that town centre redevelopment has ensured that the heart of Sutton still beats fast and positively.

In contrast, it is remarkable how little the surrounding townships have been affected; if I say that my beloved birthplace, Belmont, still exists in its own village time-warp, that is a bonus. Cheam lost its ancient farms and manor houses long before the days of tower blocks, and 1930s villagers suffered and protested twenty years before the rest of the borough. (We must not forget, though, that it was in their parish church in 1847 that a sermon was preached on the evils of the London Brighton and South Coast Railway).

To each his own: the younger generations of modern Sutton may want nothing more than their ring-roads, high-rises and shopping malls – I've grown to appreciate them myself – but I hope they will enjoy the glimpses of more leisurely days collected in this book.

The
Last Victorians

Lavender fields, Carshalton. This view is one of a series published by Stock
and Wallis of Sutton, emphasising the rural nature of the outlying areas of
the town a century ago. Fragrant reminders of the old fields occur in street
names like Lavender Road, Lavender Close, and nearby Mint Road.

High Street, junction with Benhill Street. Though shop-fronts have been modernised and merchandise changed, the upper storeys of many High Street buildings remain basically the same. Mr Stevens' butcher's shop at Norfolk House stood on the corner opposite the Grapes Hotel. Following the introduction of horse-drawn trams in the Croydon area in 1879, an electric tram route was extended to Sutton in 1906, with the terminus outside the inn.

Robin Hood Lane, looking south towards Cheam Road from the Robin Hood inn. At the turn of the century, this tree-lined lane was a peaceful way from one end of Sutton to the other. Our ancestors, walking from parish to parish, formed the ancient tracks that still cross the main lane. One of these begins behind St Nicholas' church and, leading westward via Camden Road, reaches Love Lane, Cheam, and thence to St Dunstan's church.

Throwley Road. On the right, the County School was erected on a site provided by Sutton Urban District Council, Surrey County Council making grants towards the purpose-built arts and science departments. By 1920 an increase in the number of pupils prompted expansion into Manor Park House, and eight years later a new school opened in Manor Lane. To the left of the school was the fire station and beyond, the municipal offices on the corner of High Street. The pyramid roof of the old Baptist Church tower is visible behind their roofline. None of these buildings exists today.

Sutton United Football Club. On 5 March 1898 a momentous event took place at the Robin Hood inn, when members of Sutton St Barnabas' football club and Sutton Guild Rovers football club agreed to amalgamate and be known as Sutton United. One member of the latter club that day, John J. Goossens, became Alderman Goossens, mayor of Sutton in 1938–9 and 1942–3, and was president of Sutton United at the time of its golden jubilee. Members of Sutton Guild side: left to right, standing: Adams, W. Fisher, Aldous, Spiegelhalter, H. Sharp, J. Fisher. On bench: Harrison, E. Sharp, Turner, Wood, Edwards. On ground: Goossens, Quinn.

South Metropolitan District School, Belmont. A postcard published by Belmont stationer W.H. Brain shows one of the two great influences on the development of the village. An awakening social conscience, concerned about the lost, homeless and delinquent youngsters of London 'likely to fall under the evil influences of crime, drunkenness and prostitution', led to London councils setting up industrial schools on country sites. Land on the west of the Brighton Road, Belmont, was acquired and the 'South Met' built.

The Downs School, Belmont. The 'South Met' soon needed to expand, so a separate girls' establishment was built on land between the Brighton Road and Banstead Road (later called Cotswold Road). One of the little girls sent home this photograph, taken in the gardens.

Royal Female Orphanage and St Mary's Church. The orphanage was housed in Carew Manor, Beddington, from 1866 till 1939. The first institution of its kind in the world, it had been established in Lambeth. A former pupil of Wallington Boys' school recalls how in the 1950s some 'overflow' lessons were held in the old house. Access to the main school was gained via the churchyard and lych-gate (below), thence across the fields beside the River Wandle.

All Saint's church, Carshalton. The lack of crenellations at the base of the spire caused initial doubts in identifying this church, but all other features are similar, or only slightly altered. Lettering on gravestones hereabouts has been worn away, but surnames such as Robinson, Lark and Lane can be deciphered. It is recorded that in 1891 the church was in so poor a condition that architects Sir Arthur Blomfield RA and his nephew Reginald included removal of the tower among the major changes suggested to save the building.

All Saints' Church, Benhilton, Sutton. By 1865, eighteen years after the railway reached Sutton bringing increases in prosperity and population, the town was in need of a second parish church. All Saints' was built with 874 seats, half of them free. The first incumbent, for whom the vicarage was built on an area of glebeland east of the church, was the Revd John Booker MA. In 1944, heavy enemy bombing close by destroyed the original east window of the church, severely damaged the vicarage, and completely demolished the parish hall and adjoining school.

Pit Cottages, Downs Road, Belmont. This postcard view is the best depiction of the old cottages I have ever come across. It shows on the far left part of the four cottages in existence by about 1850, built in the chalk-pit to accommodate the kiln-workers: their masters would not waste productive farmland merely to shelter the men. Later the pit was filled in and a car park and block of flats built on the site. On the far right, opposite the lamp post, is the western boundary fence of Belmont Terrace, cottages built in 1888 (contrary to law) on the common land of the Downs.

The Old Red Lion, Hackbridge Road. For more than seventy years, till the retirement of Dennis Clark in 1979, his family had held the licence of this old hostelry. Experts say that the building dates from the 1700s, and the cottages in the distance from early Victorian times.

23

Studley, Landseer Road, Sutton. The architectural style, in particular the corner turret-room, was repeated many times in houses built in this part of the town, and plenty have survived, their exteriors little altered. The road takes its name from the celebrated animal portraitist, Sir Edwin Landseer, RA, who once had a home in the area: he also designed the lions at the base of Nelson's column in Trafalgar Square.

Addison Lodge, Mulgrave Road, Sutton. Situated between Overton Road and Stanley Road, Mr Johnson's house was ideally placed. Only a short walk from the railway station, yet with southerly views of nearby open countryside, this was one of the many mansions built in the years of expansion, with city businessmen and their families in mind.

Municipal Offices, High Street, 1900–70. Sutton Urban District Council was formed in 1894, and moved into its new offices six years later, opposite Mr Ernest Shinner's rapidly expanding drapery business. The building dominated the northern corner of High Street and Throwley Road through two world wars, serving the community through borough status to London borough, until it fell to the developers' bulldozers. The three-storey replacement block of shops and offices was the first in what is now a virtually continuous northward line of modern façades on this side of the High Street.

The Chapel, St Philomena's, Carshalton. Carshalton House, a Queen Anne mansion in extensive grounds fronting onto Pound Street, was acquired in 1893 by the Daughters of the Cross. It has been a convent and girls' school ever since.

Little Woodcote. In the outer reaches of today's administrative district, in a rural atmosphere close to golf courses and woodland, this area seems to have little relevance to a London borough, but Sutton's town-dwellers should be thankful for it.

John Ruskin (1819–1900). Art critic, philosopher and social reformer, Ruskin knew this area well from boyhood: his grandmother was proprietor of an inn in Croydon. In about 1870, he came upon the spring in West Street, Carshalton, foul and rubbish-filled, and arranged for its purification. It was stocked with fish and planted with flowers, and called Margaret's Pool, in memory of his mother. His name is remembered in nearby Ruskin Road.

The
Edwardians

Sutton Green, 1902. Together with an oak tree planted by the Victoria Pond, this fountain was installed to commemorate the accession to the throne of King Edward VII, in his sixtieth year. The fountain stood at the High Street edge of the Green, but nothing remains now except a slight depression in the ground.

St Andrew's Football Club, 1904–5. The young men in the congregations of many churches formed themselves into football teams. St Andrew's was built in 1887 as a chapel of ease to serve the Wrythe area of Carshalton, accommodating 250 worshippers. This photograph was taken by F. Holloway.

Woodcote Road, Wallington. When 'Minnie' wrote to her friend in Kent on 8 March 1904, using this postcard published by Ernest A. Porter of 7 Woodcote Road, she said there were 'builders everywhere' and promised to find a prettier view next time. In the distance is the railway bridge at Wallington station, carrying the London Brighton & South Coast line, created in 1847, between Carshalton and Waddon. This road leads south to the old Woodcote estate with its famous golf course (p. 26), and to the Smitham Bottom area.

126 High Street, *c.* 1905. Left to right in the bicycle repair shop (formerly Tom Pearson's smithy) are Arthur Ayling, Harry Pearson and Fred Mortimer. The High Street (Brighton Road) was a popular route for the groups of bicyclists who rode out at weekends from London and its suburbs, to spend a few hours in the Surrey countryside. No doubt Mr Pearson's shop was a welcome sight to those who had suffered punctured tyres and other mishaps along the way. (see also p. 120)

(Sir) Noël Coward (1899–1973). In 1905, Mr and Mrs Arthur Coward with their small son Noël Pearce moved from Teddington to a villa in Lenham Road, Sutton. The little boy attended Miss Willington's school locally and made his first stage appearance, aged six, at an end-of-term concert. At that age he was already being taken to London theatres and pantomimes at Croydon, promising beginnings for a lad who would grow up to be one of the nation's most prolific and successful entertainers and composers. The family moved from Sutton to Battersea Park in 1908.

Manor Road, Wallington, 1906. In the middle distance (above) is the railway bridge already seen from Woodcote Road (p. 28), and the approach to the railway station. In the left foreground are shops and the Melbourne Hotel, with a lamp-post on the corner of Melbourne Road. Far right are the first six shops in Railway Terrace; second from the top was French and Company, photographers, who published the lower postcard view on this page. This looks in the opposite direction, with the spire of Holy Trinity parish church, dating from 1867, barely visible in the far distance.

Cock Hotel crossroads, c. 1900. On early street maps, the part of the High Street from which this photograph was taken was called the Cock Hill. It looks up to the newly built (1897) hotel and the blank end wall of shops, overlooking the gap where the old hotel had stood. Before the days of street lighting, lanterns like the Cock Hotel's lit the way for passers-by, as well as attracting them inside.

Cheam Road, 1908. This postcard view seems to have been used as a tradesman's seasonal greeting to a customer, sent from Clinton Terrace. Manor Lane. Between the trees is a glimpse of the Cock Hotel, one cycle and a horse and cart the only traffic. This really is the same spot where today vehicles hurtle loudly by. Then, pedestrians could safely cross the road by one of the sets of steps down from the raised pathways; twenty-five years later, when it was my delight to jump about on them, there was still little danger to a child.

High Street, 1907. Posted at twelve noon on Christmas Eve, this greetings card with a view of shops with their sun-blinds out hardly seems seasonal. While other parts of the High Street have undergone so much change in recent years, one finds that, though new shopfronts have been installed in this parade, almost all upper storeys remain the same. The fourth shop from the right has two large lanterns to illuminate its window displays after dark.

The Greyhound arch, High Street, *c.* 1902. Off on the far left in this snowy scene was the mouth of West Street, while far right, with a railing and bushes in front, was a residence known as Garden House. Immediately north of it, with a square wooden arch above (advertising, I believe, wagons for hire) was a footpath my family often used when visiting any friends who lived in the Carshalton direction. The Greyhound was next in the High Street, meeting-place for the local lodge of the Ancient Order of Foresters and the Independent Order of Oddfellows. On its side wall it sported a small sign claiming 'Ancient Lights' (nothing to be built to deprive it of daylight), and the plinth standing centrally above the guttering had once supported a statue of a greyhound.

An early tramcar. The Croydon to Sutton route was run by the South Metropolitan Electric Tramways and Lighting Company (SMET), which also supplied electric light to the area. The original vehicle livery was green, but changed later to red and white. The company had an office and showrooms in Sutton High Street.

The new Red Lion, High Street, *c.* 1908. For a short time in 1907, the old and the new public houses, owned by Hodgson's Kingston Brewery, stood side by side. This accounts for the empty site to the left of this picture. Who among the bystanders here would have dreamed that, in the winter of 1962–3, the real, authentic rhythm and blues sound' of a new group called the Rolling Stones, on one of their first gigs in a back room of the pub, would shatter the calm of a Friday evening.

St Anthony's Hospital, *c.* 1908. These pavilions, soon to develop into a sanatorium, were in use at St Anthony's from about 1907, in support of the fresh-air treatments promoted by the hospital. Sister Marie Thérèse founded the Daughters of the Cross in 1833 for the benefit of poor children and women prisoners. The order later founded a hospital in Düsseldorf, and then moved to England. The purpose-built hospital in London Road, North Cheam, was opened in time to take in soldiers wounded in the First World War (1914–18).

Street decorations, 1908. This type of jollification was usually mounted at Christmas time, but the inverted horseshoe design strung between posts outside the London Provincial Bank (left) and the Cock Hotel (right) was part of the town's Spring Show in this year.

Development of Belmont, 1908. From an isolated hamlet on Sutton Downs, renowned for fine air, horse-racing, prize-fighting and highway robbery, the area grew slowly but steadily. Until the mid-nineteenth century, what residents there were worked in the fields of peppermint, lavender and strawberries or at the two windmills, set on the highest points of land, with a few men labouring in the chalk pits (p. 23). The opening of the South Metropolitan School (p. 20) followed by Banstead Mental Asylum on land at Hundred Acre Farm, brought prosperity and shops and houses sprang up at the turn of the century, creating a village that has changed little since. The building far left (above) is that on the extreme right (below).

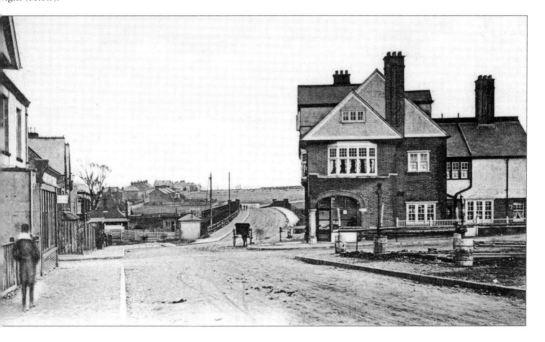

The Green, Wallington, 1908. With Manor Road (p. 30) running south from the left-hand corner, this view of Wallington Green shows Danbury Terrace, dating from about 1870, the parade of shops with sun-blinds out, and the ancient Duke's Head inn behind trees on the right.

Clergy of St Barnabas Church, 1910. Canon W. Bartlett (top left) was vicar from 1896 to 1919; he was assisted by Mr Tonge (top right) and Mr Anthony (bottom right). Many church items have been donated in memory of past members of the congregation; in 1952 Canon Bartlett was commemorated by the addition of an oak cover to the font. The fine east window was made at William Morris' studio; there is an unusual modern window designed to honour local Civil Defence workers in the Second World War.

New Police Station, Sutton

S&W. Series. 1197.

Sutton Police Station, 1909.
The town's earlier police station,
established in about 1879 was in
the High Street, adjoining Mr Dendy
Napper's bakery and steam flour mills,
which had a windmill. In 1909 these
imposing premises (above) were built
to the west of the Congregational
church in Carshalton Road, and the
old station converted into a larger
shop for Napper's. There were fifty-
six constables, nine sergeants and
one inspector on the strength of
the new station; they had their own
magistrates' court in the single-
storey building alongside. Cases had
previously been heard in the small
hall of the Public Hall in Hill Road.
This postcard view was posted only
a few days after war was declared in
August 1914. In the lower picture
mounted constables 466 and 785 are
seen in the yard behind the station.

Carshalton Ponds from the east *c.* 1905. Natural water has always abounded in this area, with millponds, watercress beds, wells, streams and pools, but the ponds have remained a focal point. Before the North Street bridge was erected in 1820, wheeled traffic forded the water (marked by the old slipway) near Honeywood, the mansion now housing Sutton's Heritage Centre. Horses were watered there, and sometimes more exotic animals, if a circus parade passed by, making its way from town to town.

Maldon Road, Wallington, looking west. This residential road was one of a number linking Bute Road and Manor Road, its houses built for businessmen and their families who, with the railway station nearby and green spaces not far off, could enjoy the best of both worlds. The spire of the parish church of Holy Trinity can be seen in the middle distance; standing on the corner of the main road, it was consecrated in 1867.

Culvers Bridge. The
River Wandle divides
north of the Hack
Bridge creating Culvers
Island, named after the
nearby Victorian house
which stood till after the
Second World War and
the eighteenth-century
mill, two of whose
stones are displayed
at Millside, off Culvers
Avenue.

The Wandle at Beddington. In pre-mechanical power days, water-driven industries abounded along the river with mills
treating lavender, camomile, peppermint and other herbs, and producing snuff, leather, oils, paper and textiles. Local names
such as Vellum Drive recall those thriving times when there was work for many people near their homes. The Wandle joins
the Thames at Wandsworth.

Sutton Green, from Bushey Road. Following the Enclosure Act of 1809, a part of Sutton Common that came to be called The Green was given to the parish. Successive drawings and photographs indicate that the borders of that piece of land have remained unchanged though a variety of boundary marks, from bushes to chestnut-paling fences, have been noted. Generations of children have played there, while funfairs, circuses and political meetings have made use of the open space. In the 1930s, Oswald Mosley held a rally there for members of his New Party (British Fascists). The Coronation fountain (left) is visible in the middle distance.

Footpath beside the Angel cutting, looking towards The Green. The story goes that the Prince Regent, who became King George IV in 1820, often travelled by coach to Brighton along this road. He was concerned at his horses' suffering as they struggled up the hill (Benhill – probably 'where beans grow') toward the end of their twelve-mile half of the journey: fresh horses were waiting at the Cock Inn. He ordered that a new road on level ground be cut through, close to the Angel Inn. A footbridge was added, from which there used to be a delightful view across the treetops.

Coronation day, 1911, in the High Street. On 6 May 1910 at fifteen minutes to midnight, King Edward VII died after only nine years as sovereign; he was succeeded by his oldest surviving son, George. It was more than a year later – Thursday 22 June 1911 – when the King and his Queen (Mary, formerly Princess May of Teck) were crowned in Westminster Abbey. There was rejoicing throughout the land. Here are some of the good folk of Sutton, with band playing, flags flying and the gentry in their carriages, approaching the crossroads at the Cock Hotel (sign on the wall far left – see p. 31). The shops identified behind the Union Flag are Watts (greengrocer) and Riddington's Bakery ('general caterers') with stables at the rear, where my grandfather tended the delivery-van horses. After the Second World War the stables site was used for civil defence emergency training; it is now part of the entrance to Safeway. In the distance, the corner shop on the right was Wootton Brothers' draper's shop. Mr Robert Wootton used to stand in the shop doorway greeting customers, always with a bunch of violets in his coat lapel. He had these from the flower-seller whose pitch was on the corner of Grove Road, but never paid her for them. Instead, each winter he gave her a new overcoat.

Carshalton Park, open to the public. On 25 June 1913, the Lord Lieutenant of Surrey officially opened the 19-acre park on land purchased by the local authority, south of Ruskin Road. Note the little human drama that seems to be developing, with the casual behaviour of the three young men in the foreground apparently giving concern to some of their elders on the platform. This is taken from a commemorative postcard published by Stock and Wallis of 174 High Street, Sutton.

War and Peace (I)

The Drive, Nonsuch Park, 1914. Many had come along this road through the park, riding hard in times of trouble: messengers during the Civil War; Samuel Pepys, diarist and civil servant, taking vital papers to safety in the palace when first the Plague and then the Great Fire raged in London; Barbara Villiers' son by King Charles II bringing a gang of bullies to lay claim to the land. Now a solitary cyclist contemplates news of another conflict, the 'war to end wars' – but it did not.

The new church at Belmont. Consecrated by the Bishop of Southwark on 23 December 1915, the church's foundation stone had been laid on 18 July 1914 (above), after a procession from the 'tin church' in Downs Road, which thereafter became the church hall. The first vicar of the new church was the Revd A.E. Tonkin. The lower picture was taken before houses were built in Northdown Road (then a track leading west to the Northey estate and Kerr's farm), although the landowners had engaged Mr Belcher ten years before to plant trees. Opposite the church on the corner of Station Road and Avenue Road were the tall houses with shops put up 'on spec' some twenty years before. First in Avenue Road was the infants' and juniors' school, built in 1902 to accommodate one hundred and fifty children, next door to that the Belmont Laundry, and then the bungalows and houses that eventually stretched as far north as Dorset Road. The bypass road was not made till about 1928, and there was open land with a few houses all the way to Burdon Lane.

A Greeting from SUTTON.

GOD BLESS YOU AND PROTECT YOU.

ABSENT ON DUTY! Yet with us every moment, in our Thoughts and Prayers.

A wartime greeting. One of the 'Pro Patria' series, this embossed postcard was sent with a birthday message to 'dear Edie' from her friend in April 1915. Flags of the then Allies include (far left) Japan and (third from right) Italy. These morale-boosters were intended primarily for despatch to soldiers away from home.

A wartime schoolboy. This young lad was a pupil at Banstead Road School, Belmont, built in 1896 to accommodate one hundred and fifty boys and girls. The Labour Certificate procedure was in place at the time, by which any schoolchild not less than twelve years of age, having attained the standard required by the local authority, could leave school 'to be beneficially employed'. This was a boon to soldiers' families, as it released boys to earn money to augment what the army paid, and girls to stay at home and help with the younger children. This eleven-year-old proudly wore on his coat lapel regimental insignia to honour his older brother, fighting in France. I do not know the significance of the floral decoration – perhaps for a wedding? I never asked the man this boy grew into, though there were countless opportunities: he was my father.

Sutton station. The London Brighton & South Coast Railway reached Sutton in 1847, when the line was extended from West Croydon to Epsom. A sermon was preached at Cheam, denouncing the shattering of Sunday peace. Wealthy businessmen brought their families to the comparative countryside of the area; they became the first commuters, their numbers increasing till a new station was necessary (1883). In January 1901, the royal train, bringing Queen Victoria's coffin from the Isle of Wight to her funeral, passed through Sutton. Electrification of the line began in 1909, but wartime shortages of materials caused postponement of completion till 1925.

Cheam Road, looking west. The attractive street lamp and style of men's and women's dress date this postcard at around the time of the First World War. It was sent from Sutton (Surrey) to an address in Sutton near Hull on 5 July 1917, and shows a quiet rural setting of the main road to Cheam that is hard to imagine, given today's volume of traffic.

Benfleet Hall War Hospital. One of a series published by Stock and Wallis, this postcard was sent by Lance-Corporal Taylor to staff and patients in the Red Cross Hospital, Stoke-on-Trent, on 24 April 1918. The wounded men depicted are dressed in the shapeless blue suits, white shirts, red neckties and regimental headgear which together earned them the affectionate nickname 'blue boys'.

Disaster at Benfleet Hall. The hall had been the home of Mr Hogg and stood in Benhill Road, on the triangle of land now occupied by Benfleet Close. Young Adrian Holme climbed up to pose on the roof with firemen called to a blaze.

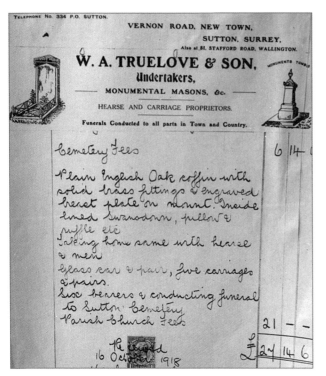

Funeral account, 1918*. Messrs Truelove's, funeral directors, had two addresses at the time the above bill was tendered. It is interesting to note the inclusion of 'New Town' in the Sutton one, since development on the Carshalton side of the town had begun more than fifty years before. The cemetery at Sutton Common (below) was administered by Sutton Urban District Council, and the fees shown here included the purchase of exclusive rights of burial (four guineas) and a charge of £1 4s 0d for grave-digging.

J. Huggett and Son, Station Road, Belmont, 1918. A fourteen-year-old girl, having passed all her business studies examinations at evening classes, was employed by Mr Huggett at 15s a week, 8 to 5 Monday to Friday and 8 to 1 Saturdays, to run his office. It seems her duties included stoking the office stove; one day it back-fired and she was overcome by smoke, only the timely arrival of a customer saving her from suffocation.

The rescuer of the girl mentioned above was local resident and world-famous viola player Lionel Tertis. When not travelling the country giving concerts to raise funds for war charities, he served as a War Reserve policeman, patrolling the district or guarding Sutton Water Company's Ventnor Road reservoir, where he took the opportunity to rehearse, to the delight of passers-by.

A family portrait, 1919. A few days before Easter 1919, fourteen-year-old Edie (standing, right) planned a surprise for her parents: Dada had just returned after fighting in France in the First World War. The younger children, Winnie (standing left), Henley (standing centre), Lily (with doll) and Hughie (with ball), were smuggled into the studio of Mr Nesbitt the photographer at 88 High Street, Sutton, where they posed for this picture. Unfortunately, their absence had been noticed and they were met by their frantic father as they walked home, and all was revealed.

Peace celebration, Malden Road, Cheam, 1919. Soldiers, civilians, clergy, Boy Scouts, children are all gathered on a vacant corner site to give thanks for the end of four years of war. The houses are on the north side of Lumley Road, the distant chimney between them was at Cheam brickworks, and the trees far right near the top of Church Hill. A shop – Marsh's newsagents and sweetshop – and a petrol station stood on this site in the 1930s.

St Nicholas Parish Church. This church was built in 1863–4 at a cost of £7,200, on the site of a small medieval church in which attempts had been made (by the addition of a gallery) to accommodate Sutton's fast-growing population. In 1893 the vestry was added on the north side, costing a further £1,400, and at the same time new altar rails and a north porch were provided, and the heating improved. The reverse of the original postcard from which this view is taken had been used as a sort of diary, detailing a young girl's day out with friends in 1921, walking from Mitcham to Sutton with 'lunch at Riddington's 12.30 to 2.15 o/c'.

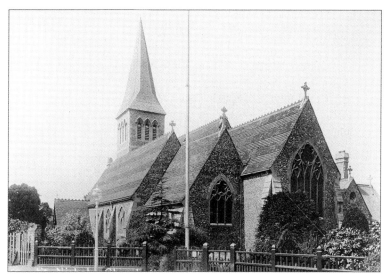

West Street, Sutton, 1920s. One of the town's oldest streets, it ran from the High Street to Robin Hood Lane, having evolved from the original track between parish churches via Camden Road and Love Lane (p. 18). Just round the corner from Herrington's (p. 55) was a permanent covered market; in the 1930s, I remember, there was one stall I always made straight for: it had caged birds, pet rabbits, and other small animals. West Street Primary School opened in about 1860, more than twenty years before attendance was made compulsory. On a bend in the road in Victorian times was a pond known as Divers Ditch, a link in the line of natural water sources to which man's earliest settlements can be traced.

An aerial view of Sutton town centre, before 1921. The High Street can be readily followed on this postcard view, from the railway station at top centre (with lines going east) down to the Cock Hotel and the shop at right angles, built on the site of the old hotel (p. 31). To the left of the picture at that level, the police station on the old Sutton Court land has hardly changed in eighty years. The whole terrace of shops down to Throwley Road is there, with the Municipal Offices (demolished 1970) on the lower corner. The gap in the building line near the lower left-hand corner awaits the development of the Surrey County cinema. Three church towers are prominent: the Baptist Church facing the High Street was demolished in 1934 to make way for part of Mr Ernest Shinner's expanding department store. Local Baptists built a new church in Cheam Road. The tall pale tower marks out Trinity Methodists' Church, which has stood since 1909 on the east corner of Cheam Road, and the parish church of St Nicholas is seen in the bottom right-hand corner, with vast garage roofs including those of Surrey Motors' Speedway House (1912–60) in St Nicholas Road, to its left.

The '20s

Christ Church, Sutton, 1923. Nina Washford, standing left, and her older sister Edith (in dark dress, seated right) were two of the team of Girls' Friendly Society members who did the gold threadwork and other embroidery on their crimson banner. The society was founded in 1875 within the Church of England by Mrs Mary Townsend. It aimed to offer spiritual support, friendship and recreation to young women, in particular those who, for family or work reasons, had to live away from home.

Love Lane, Cheam. (titled 'Lovers Walk' by the publisher of this postcard). This path, running roughly parallel and to the east of Cheam Road, leads past Boney Hole, where once a bourne would occasionally rise through the Thanet sand, till the water company built a pumping station nearby. It is easy with an adult's mind to realise how the sinister nickname arose, but as a little child I dreaded passing the spot, expecting to see a skeleton. Those walking towards Cheam are treated to an unusual aspect of St Dunstan's Church (right, in the distance). The fence on the left marked the boundary of Mrs Seear's property The Quarry, while the iron railings edged land later to become Seears Park.

Floral tributes, Carshalton, 1921. A note on the reverse of this anonymous photograph gives the date of burial as 24 January 1921, grave number 30/8, and the location 'along by the wall in the new ground'.

Herrington's, men's outfitters. This was on the south-east corner of High Street and West Street, the shop formerly occupied by Odd and Sons' sports store, which stocked the world-famous cricket bats made at their factory nearby. Where possible, the willow used was gathered locally, on the banks of the Pyl brook not far away. Herrington's at different times had shops at various High Street addresses, with services ranging from furniture and carpet suppliers to pawnbroking.

First Sutton Scout Troop, 1925. The details on the two pages of this spare-time activities record card speak for themselves.

Wallington Girls' School. When it opened on 23 October 1926, in premises in Stanley Park Road, Miss Wallace was headmistress of the school. She retired in 1937. The box-pleated gym slip with blouse, and thick black stockings, were normal schoolgirl wear in winter (above), replaced by cotton frocks and panama hats in summer (left).

Chemistry laboratory, Sutton County School A set of postcards (of which this view is one) was published to mark the opening of the purpose-built school for boys in Manor Lane, under headmaster Mr J.A. Cockshutt. Costing over £45,000 in 1928, the school could accommodate five hundred pupils, more than it had been able to cope with at Throwley Road (p. 19) or Manor Park (p. 82).

Wolf Cubs' cricket match. The 4th Sutton played 3rd Sutton pack on Saturday 9 June 1928 at Collingwood Road recreation ground, Sutton. At the back: Miss Gibbs (Cubmaster); back row, left to right: Goodison, Baker, Hutchinson, Green, Cowell, Williams junior, Webb senior; front row: Edser, Piper, Boreham junior, Webb junior, Billinghurst, Boreham senior, King, Laverick. The 3rd Sutton pack beat the 4th by 48 to 36 runs and the second innings was cancelled: 'rain stopped play'.

Parish church of St Dunstan, Cheam. Published by A. Ainsworth, stationer, when his address was 20 Malden Road (changed to The Broadway on road-widening in 1934), this postcard shows the church interior before the main walls were panelled and the chancel walls and ceiling colour-washed. The text over the chancel steps, 'Serve the Lord in fear and rejoice unto him with reverence', was also obliterated at some stage. The present building replaced an earlier church in 1864, being erected further north, leaving the old chancel (Lumley chapel, p. 88) standing in the graveyard. Canon H. Wesley Dennis was rector of Cheam 1917–38.

Malden Road (Station Road), Cheam, *c.* 1926. As the General single-decker bus prepared to move off towards North Cheam en route for Raynes Park, there was sufficient traffic to explain why, within six years, this road would be fully widened and re-named The Broadway. A few of the lovely old trees from the Cheam House estate survived, and at that time the old bakery (the single-storey building protruding in the distance) had not been demolished. Hidden behind the bus is the Old Cottage (p. 106) serving as Cheam Parish Council offices, having been moved from its original position nearer the crossroads in 1922.

A happy birthday, Belmont, 1925. Baby
Violet, clearly thrilled with her new
rocking-horse, has her first ride in the
backyard. Her big brothers Henley and
Hughie had walked up from Sutton
carrying Dobbin between them. Three-
quarters of a century later, he is still a
cherished member of the family.

Sharing out the bridal flowers,
Monday 29 August 1926. Behind
the bride's family home
(3 Banstead Road, Belmont) was
Overton's Field, where the wedding
group had been photographed.
During the First World War, troops
were encamped on the land. In
1929–30, Sutton and Cheam
General Hospital (pp. 61, 68) was
built on the northern part. The
fence in the background here
marks the boundary of The Downs
children's department (p. 20).

V. Coppen's, Waterloo House, 169–75 High Street, Sutton. If dressmakers and housewives could not find what they wanted in the drapery department of Shinner's, Coppen's would come to the rescue. Advertisements claimed they were 'the up-to-date draper' – 'Always replete with the latest novelties and seasonable goods'. There was something comfortable and timeless about Coppens' – staff, stock, surroundings – that I as a small girl preferred to the bright sophistication of Shinner's. Close inspection will reveal a number of interesting signs and advertisements in the vicinity.

Grove Road, looking east. A century ago, the trees that suggested the street-name grew at regular intervals (as seen on the left) for the length of the road, on both sides. The kerb curving out of the picture on the left marks the corner of Sutton Park Road. The tall, square-fronted building is the telephone exchange, opened in about 1928, with the more ornately designed General Post Office nearer the camera.

The Angel, *c.* 1925. The hedges in the lower corners of this postcard indicate where the cutting went through Angel Hill, to make the level road in use since Regency times (p. 40). Remains of the steep old turnpike road still exist on either side. To the right of the picture, Rose Hill leads towards the eight-hundred-acre site developed 1928–35 by London County Council as the St Helier estate, to re-house inner-city families. Modern interpretation of the old inn's name has resulted in a sign with a striped fish!

Foundations of the General Hospital, Belmont, 1930. The site for Sutton and Cheam General Hospital (p. 68) overlooked the junction of Brighton, Banstead and Chiltern Roads, and local residents pottered around the footings at weekends.

Lower High Street, Sutton. I have always thought that this part of High Street had the feel of a separate village, perhaps because of its proximity to The Green (top left, behind the trees), and because it has its own inn, the Cricketers (on the right), parts of which could be well over 200 years old. Formerly with Nalder & Collyer's brewery, in 1936 it became one of Ind Coope's group. Severely damaged by enemy bombs in the Second World War, it survived to become one of Sutton's older landmarks.

Sutton High School hockey field, 1920s. At this time the girls had to go elsewhere to play hockey and cricket, although netball and tennis could be accommodated in the school grounds. A number of former pupils have been consulted, and th consensus of opinion is that the field was in Gander Green Lane. Miss Margaret Chalmers Whyte opened the school on 1 January 1884 with eighty pupils and a staff of seven. Within fifteen months, girls were sitting public examinations, an in 1897 the first university place was won. Over the years a number of extensions and alterations have been made, and i 1984 a sports hall was created at the Cheam Road premises.

The
Thriving '30s

Plaza cinema, Carshalton Road, 1934. This was one of Sutton's two main cinemas built after the First World War, the other was the Surrey County. Cheam Road picture theatre had opened in 1911, and earlier movie houses included the Hippodrome in Carshalton Road, the Electric Theatre and the basement-level Bio-Picture Hall, both in High Street. The Plaza was renamed the Granada, demolished in 1979, and Sutton Park House is now on the site. The County became the Gaumont, replaced in 1959 by W.H. Smith's bookshop, and only the Cheam Road building survives, called in turn the Curzon, Studio 1-2-3, and Legends. When the Plaza celebrated its first birthday, patrons were invited to stir a huge bowl of fruit-cake mix on display in the foyer. After baking, slices of the cake would be handed out. My father would not let me eat any of the cake because he had witnessed a man dropping cigarette ash into the mixture as he stirred.

4th Sutton Scout troop. It is summer camp 1935, venue unknown. Though most of the young men remain unidentified, at least one in the back row has already appeared in this book, as a Wolf Cub on p. 57.

Recreation ground, Malden Road, Cheam. The northern part of Cheam Park, once the site of funfairs for Sunday School outings (p. 74), was later laid out formally with tennis courts, a pool for model boat-sailing, and colourful flower-beds. From the time of Queen Victoria royal occasions have been celebrated there, and the surrounding parkland has made an ideal venue for rallies and civic events.

The Rectory, Cheam. This lovely old house had been the home of successive Rectors of Cheam for more than three hundred years when this postcard view was taken. Canon Herbert Wesley Dennis MA was rector then, succeeded by the Revd William Samuel Hayman MA who, with his wife and daughter Angela, played host to the people of the village at garden parties and fêtes before the Second World War.

Cheam Broadway, 1930. The proprietor of Crossways Pharmacy believed in catching his customers young, when he took this cheery snapshot outside his premises.

65

Mrs Rowe, Cheam newsagent and confectioner
1932. My childhood recollection of this shop,
visited weekly to pick up my *Chicks' Own*
(from which Mother taught me to read!), later
Crackers, Film Fun and *Girls' Crystal*, was the
mighty step up into the dark interior, and Mrs
Rowe's patience when you had a whole penny
to spend and a whole counterful of sweets to
choose from. This building, on the corner of
The Broadway and Park Lane, was part of
the complex area of cottages, bakehouse and
cartshed which had to be cut back in order to
widen the road.

Belmont Church and war memorial. Every city, town and village in the land erected some kind of monument after the First
World War, to commemorate those of their own people who died in the conflict. At the junction of Station Road and Queen
Road, the site chosen for Belmont's memorial would then have been a quiet, eminently suitable place, close to the parish
church, with room for those large poppy wreaths to accumulate each 11 November, then known as Armistice Day.

Mr Shinner's arcade, High Street to Throwley Road. In the 1930s, this was a favourite spot for many children on any visit to Sutton. There were some good shops: one sold artists' materials and framed pictures, another had a window crammed with colourful china knick-knacks. The milliner, with hats labelled 'As worn by Joan Crawford/Greer Garson/Judy Garland' and other film stars, always caught the eye. Halfway down on the right were steps leading to a side entrance of Woolworth's, but best of all was the great echoing sound one little girl could make by running full-tilt from Throwley Road to the High Street, singing loudly – but only if the attendant wasn't there.

Lunchtime in Belmont, 1930. The men of the family could spare a moment for the camera before returning to work. The dog Spot joined this group in the back garden at 40 Kings Road.

St Dunstan's parish church, Cheam. 'He giveth his beloved sleep' is carved above the lych-gate, leading into the graveyard. The purpose of such gates was to shelter the funeral parties while they awaited the priest to lead the cortège into church. 'Lych' comes from an old English word for 'corpse'. On the right is the path leading past the surviving chalk-block wall of the stables of West Cheam Manor, which was demolished in the eighteenth century. Through the middle opening of the gate one can see part of the south wall of the Lumley chapel (p. 88) that had been the chancel of the earlier church.

Sutton and Cheam General Hospital, Belmont. This view of the new hospital was published by Rex's, newsagents on the corner of Brighton Road and Downs Road. Sir Alan Garrett Anderson KBE performed the opening ceremony on 30 September 1931, and the original accommodation was for twenty-two male, twenty-two female, twelve private patients and twelve children.

Tabor School, Cheam, Published by Mr Knott of Cheam Library, 1 High Street, this postcard shows part of what claimed to be one of the earliest private preparatory schools in the country. It was built for Dr Daniel Sanxay in 1719, though it had its beginnings half a century earlier, when one Mr George Aldrich moved into Whitehall – possibly fleeing from London and the Great Plague – with a number of boy pupils. Headmasters came and went till 1855, when Mr R.S. Tabor bought the school and local people began to call it by his name. Many former pupils came to prominence in later life, with Prince Philip of Greece most readily recalled, now HRH the Duke of Edinburgh, consort to our Queen.

Joan Watts' School of Dancing, 1936. Miss Watts (far left) had forty-eight pupils at this time, all taking part in this finale, for which the girls' dresses were green net and satin, with candy-pink trimmings. Proceeds of the concert were sent to Carshalton Hospital. Classes were held at Miss Watts' home at 99 Carshalton Park Road, and later at her studio, above the parade of shops in Beynon Road. Several pupils went on to become teachers, and some were engaged by ballet companies or dance troupes.

Brock's Fireworks. In 1901 the pyrotechnic manufacturers moved from their premises in Selhurst to Gander Green Lane, Sutton. To reduce the risk of fire or explosions spreading should an accident occur, work was carried out in small sheds scattered over a wide area of old Cheam Common. Workers handling powders and explosives wore black overalls, while those engaged in packing and despatching fireworks wore white. For many years the company had been responsible for spectacular displays to celebrate important events, especially those presented at the Crystal Palace. There was a serious side to the work: during the First World War a younger member of the family, Commander Frank Arthur Brock, helped design a bullet 'so sensitive it will ignite and explode on impact with the thin fabric of the Zeppelin's outer skin'. Its use prevented many enemy machines reaching their targets in London and the south. He was killed in the raid on Zeebrugge on St George's day 1918.

St Helier Hospital. Built in 1937–8 on the south-east part of Rosehill Park, the hospital's main entrance was in Wrythe Lane. Its initial capacity was over seven hundred beds, compared with the earlier general hospital, Sutton and Cheam (p. 68), opened only six years before with a mere sixty-eight beds. John Roy Major, Prime Minister 1990–7, was born here on 29 March 1943.

Station Road, Belmont, 1934. Generally agreed to have been a highly successful publicity exercise, the people who marketed Hugon's Atora beef suet had vans drawn by pairs of bullocks delivering their goods. One day they arrived in Belmont, and everyone got to work with their Brownie cameras to record the strange visitors as they drew up outside the shop of Mr Jones the draper.

Nonsuch County School for Girls, 1937. Schemes for a new girls' school for the area were first proposed in 1914, but the land assigned was later acquired by Southern Railway. When a site in the south-east corner of Nonsuch Park was decided on, the first sod was cut on Wednesday 30 December 1936. The architects were Jarvis and Richards. The driveway of the finished school (above) was at right angles to Ewell Road, close by Harefield Bridge; below is a group of the men who built the school.

Nonsuch mansion, 1930s. The first house on this site was built in about 1731 for Joseph Thompson, and incorporated into the present house (above) designed for Mr Samuel Farmer seventy years later by Jeffrey Wyatt, who went on to reconstruct Windsor Castle. Nonsuch gardens, already famous for their magnificent trees and the lilacs believed to be descendants of the first six 'lelack' trees to grow in England, were enhanced by successive owners. The mansion was acquired by the local authority in 1937, but little was done to attract visitors: one room was kept open for the sale of ice-cream, and the house was advertised as available for wedding receptions and parties. In 1991 there was talk of converting the park into a golf course and concerned people formed themselves into the Friends of Nonsuch, who have ever since been promoting the cause of the house and its grounds.

Cheam Park House, *c.* 1930. This elegant house was destroyed in a Second World War enemy air attack, having for one hundred and forty years dominated the park after which it was named. Several generations of the family of London tea merchant Mr A. Palmer lived there. In 1826 Mr Palmer donated land to the north of the estate for the building of the National School for boys (demolished in 1993). In summer, swings and merry-go-rounds were set up in the area for the enjoyment of children on their annual day's outings from London (p. 64). Sutton and Cheam Borough Council acquired the estate in 1937. The bushes in the foreground of this photograph concealed a ha-ha, a protective fence erected in a ditch, so that the view from the house was not spoiled by unsightly railings.

Cock Hotel crossroads, *c.* 1933. This is the crossroads as I first remember the area, where one changed buses on frequent family journeys between Cheam and Belmont. Favourite items were the giant eye-glasses high on the timbered façade of the optician's premises, the telephone kiosk outside the picture theatre, and the neon-lighting 'lucky charms' on the outer walls of the theatre. It was unfortunate that they took the form of swastikas, the hated symbol of Nazi Germany, so had to be removed as war approached. There was always the smell of coffee coming from the grinders in the shop window close by the optician's, and it was fun to watch the policeman directing traffic. Not till about 1936 were traffic lights installed here. The heaviest flow of vehicles I ever saw on this stretch of road was in 1938, when many families packed up and fled from the danger areas of London, fearing that war and air raids were imminent.

Charter
Celebrations

Borough status notice, 1934. Sutton's population of fewer than 1,200 in 1801, had reached more than 75,000 by 1934 and, as the Lord Mayor's message of September 1934 says: 'it has developed very rapidly in recent years'. There was great rejoicing when the new borough was proposed and four days of celebration planned, encompassing twenty-six events.

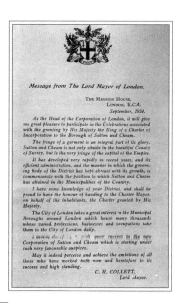

Coat of arms. The borough's new coat of arms incorporated four crosses, signifying association with the Archbishopric of Canterbury, two keys for its Domesday link with Chertsey Abbey, a popinjay from the arms of the Lumley family, once major landowners, and the motto of Dr Hacket, Cheam's courageous rector during the Commonwealth.

The Charter Mayor. Councillor Sidney Horatio Marshall,
Justice of the Peace and County Councillor, of Bracklin,
56 The Crescent, Belmont, was chosen to be charter
mayor. He was the donor of the silver chain (below) which,
encased in pure gold, with solid gold badge enamelled
with the new coat of arms (p. 75), was to be worn by all
mayors of the borough.

The Charter Mayoress. Mr Marshall's mayoress was his sister, here wearing the silver-gilt and enamelled jewel, on a silver-gilt chain. This item of borough insignia was unique in being the only one not donated by an individual: it was the gift of the women's associations of Sutton and Cheam, to be worn by all mayoresses.

The Charter Town Clerk. The town clerk's wig and robes, as worn here by the charter town clerk, Mr Harry Bolton, MBE, were a gift to the borough from a former member of the old Sutton Urban District Council, Mr E. Morris Gibson.

The Charter Mayor in Belmont.* The mayor stops the traffic at the foot of his own road (The Crescent), to the obvious delight of his friends and neighbours. In the background are the corner windows of Mr Jones the draper. Far left by the car is the Bearer of the Mace, which was given to the borough by Sir Edward J. Holland JP, DL, CA. It was an impressive item of silver encased in pure gold (left).

St Anthony's Hospital.* The charter celebrations coincided with the thirtieth anniversary of the founding of the hospital. During the procession round the new borough, which preceded the presentation of the charter in Manor Park, Sutton, a halt was called so that commemorative photographs could be taken on the steps of the hospital (above). The mayor also inspected a detachment of the local fire brigade, with the mace bearer (far right) in attendance.

Charter events. The programme included an air display, a football match (kick-off by local philanthropist and one-time secretary of the Football Association Sir Frederick Wall), in which Sutton United beat Queens Park Rangers 4–2, a jamboree of youth, a civic ball, firework display and funfair, procession of decorated vehicles, beating the bounds, a children's film show and tea-party at which ten thousand lemonades were dispensed. Mrs Bethell allowed the presentation of a pageant in the grounds of her home Cheam Park (p. 74) on 13 and 14 September. In eight episodes, with a huge cast of local actors, singers, dancers, horsemen and musicians, the history of Sutton and Cheam was told. One entire family of six, adults and children, took part; they were our next-door neighbours, and we were there to cheer them on.

War and Peace (II)

A corner of Delmont, 1940s. Tell-tale signs of the precautions that needed to be taken for safety in the black-out included kerbs painted white, likewise the running-board and bumper of the car. Seldom was anyone seen in the street without some sort of haversack or other bag to hold one's gas-mask. The man thus kitted out and standing on the corner of Belmont Road was a member of the National Fire Service on picket duty.

Manor Park, 1939. When school parties from Cheam came by bus for swimming lessons at Throwley Road baths, they could take a handy short-cut from the Plaza bus stop, through the park. In the Second World War, a large underground public air-raid shelter was dug towards the eastern boundary near the Central Library, which had formerly housed a boys' school. Open-air entertainments were also presented in wartime in that part of the park. The 1921 memorial was erected following the First World War, by public subscription, to a design by J.S.W. Burmester RIBA. The original area set aside for the memorial was enlarged in 1931.

JEA Home Guard unit, 1940. Having taken over responsibility for the supply of electricity to the town, the JEA found itself engaged in many extra duties in wartime. On at least one occasion electrician plumber-joiner Corporal Ernie Hennessy (far left) and jointer's mate Jack Laws (second from right) were the targets for machine-gunfire from enemy aircraft, as they cycled off in answer to yet another emergency call.

Old Post Office, Beddington. Damaged by an enemy V1 flying bomb in 1944 and demolished five years later, this ancient building (possibly from the Tudor period) stood on the corner of Guy Road and Church Lane. At different times it was divided into smaller units, one serving as the Post office, and another (left) as a shop selling R. White's ale and ginger beer (advertisement on end wall posters).

Girl Guide. Scouts and Guides were encouraged to wear uniform whenever possible; it inspired confidence and gave the older ones some feeling of responsibility when they carried out small tasks like carrying messages. They were well organised with salvage collections, growing vegetables and fruit, baby-sitting to release mothers for war-work, and fund-raising. In recognition of what they had accomplished, a rally was held in Cheam Park, attended by the Chief Guide, Lady Olave Baden-Powell. The Shamrock patrol of 1st Belmont Guides took with them their knitted mascot Katy, and were bursting with pride when the Chief Guide stopped and spoke to them about her.

Pets in wartime. Sisters-in-law Edith and Ada standing in the front garden of 13 Pelton Avenue, Belmont. It was not only humans whose food was curtailed by wartime restrictions. Jock the Scottish terrier was served up some very un-dog-type meals from time to time. Ada's budgerigar Peter (who could recite his name and address, and picked up some unkind words about the enemy from hearing his 'Mother's' oft-repeated response to the air-raid sirens) needed imported seed; when supplies ran out there were no substitutes, and he died.

Victory Parades. Passing the saluting base in Grove Road (above) is the Civil Defence (Air Raid Precautions) contingent in the procession to celebrate the end of the war in Europe. Townspeople lined the route, showing their appreciation of the sterling work done by the emergency services during some appalling enemy air-attacks. Another celebration took place at Sutton United's football field, Gander Green Lane, Sutton, where Mrs Marjorie Barnes, Women's Voluntary Service centre organiser, led her contingent in the parade, preceded by Civil Defence workers and followed by fire-fighters (below). In the background, among others facing the stands, are units of the Home Guard (Local Defence Volunteers), Sea Rangers, Boy Scouts and nurses. Other official celebrations included a children's fête in the recreation ground with a baby show, fancy dress competition, Punch and Judy, pony rides and model railway rides.

Sutton United annual dinner, 1946. Recovering from wartime difficulties, the club had one of its most successful years, winning the Athenian League championship 6–0 against Barking in the final and the Surrey Senior Cup when they beat Woking in the final. Here, President Councillor John J. Goossens (left – see p. 19) re-lives the Athenian game with Sutton's Mayor Alderman H.J. Trickett (right), watched by club chairman Stanley Ruddle. This was the year that produced Sutton's first home-bred England international in Charlie Vaughan, who was signed by Charlton Athletic.

Creation of Sutton's parliamentary constituency. Until 1946 Sutton had been part of the Epsom (Mid-Surrey) constituency. With the population rising, reorganisation of the system called for the election of Sutton's own MP. He was County Alderman Sidney Horatio Marshall of Belmont, in which village he was held in high regard, having been first elected to St John the Baptist parish Church council in 1921. He was chairman of Sutton Urban District Council in 1933–4, and Charter Mayor in 1934 (p. 76). He was knighted in 1952 and two years later applied for the Manor of the Chiltern Hundreds and retired from politics. He died in 1973 in his ninetieth year; his home in The Crescent was demolished some time later and Patricia Gardens developed on the site.

Farewell Bobbie, 1946. Food shortages continued for some time after the war ended. Families with gardens grew fruit and vegetables and kept chickens and rabbits, to supplement their diet. While no-one makes a pet of a cabbage, parting from a favourite bunny was always sad.

5a Cotswold Road, Belmont, 1948. There was a severe housing shortage immediately after the war, with many homes lost through enemy bombing and a lack of materials with which to re-build. Reflected in the front-room window of their half-a-house are two of the three adults who lived in the downstairs part of what had been a farm-worker's cottage; a newly-married couple occupied the upstairs rooms.

St John's Church choir, Belmont. Like so many long-established groups, the choir had been severely depleted during the war. In the late 1940s, organist and choir-master William Bigsby introduced female voices by recruiting some thirty girl singers from local schools and from the church fellowship choral group. Funds for their new blue robes were raised by concerts and other events, but at first they did not have enough for everyone. The girls were formed into two units and each robe shared. A robing vestry was contrived for them in the organ loft. In the 1960s almost one hundred people were actively involved in the music of the church, including ten organists.

The Lumley chapel, Cheam. When I attended Sunday school at St Dunstan's, before and during the Second World War, I thought the chapel a sad old building. Even when, during later air raids, we held our little services in a small building near the chapel, no-one told us of its history. When major refurbishment took place, its unique contents and decoration were revealed. This photograph of part of Lady Lumley's tomb, which dates from late Tudor times, was found among my late cousin's collection, taken to record our local heritage. The carvings are thought to include a depiction of a garden at Nonsuch Palace.

After Austerity

(Sir) Harry Secombe. A much-loved and respected resident of Sutton in the 1950s and '60s, he had a house on the west corner of Cheam Road and York Road, where centuries before a tollgate had stood. Carlton House and Wrighton Court now occupy the site, but to some of us it will always be 'Secombe corner', as the bus conductors used to call out. Sir Harry patronised many local organisations including the cricket club (with its ground almost opposite), St Helier Hospital League of Friends, and the Scout troop to which his son belonged. Here he is, larking about, accompanied by the late Mr Ron Ockenden, at a sports day (not Sutton).

St Andrew's Presbyterian Church, Cheam. The church in Northey Avenue had its own Brownie pack, which in 1951 urgently needed adult help. The writer, given the courtesy title of Tawny Owl, and Greta Hughes, a member of the congregation (seen here with the little girls), kept the group going, meeting each week in the church hall. Highlight of their time with the pack was a bus journey to Sutton, where a tea-party in the Granada restaurant was followed by a visit to the pantomime.

Ewell Road, Cheam. Shops in this parade include the Cheam Bazaar, Mr Pinnegar the butcher, Mr Chamberlain the vet, a dress shop, the Cheam Hall (hired out for dances, parties and wedding receptions) and the Co-op. Bus stops served the 408/470 routes. Just out of the picture (bottom right-hand corner) was the United Dairies depot, so no doubt the horse was picking up his stride for those last few yards home.

Actor Jimmy Hanley (1918–70). Jimmy lived for some time in the Sutton Common Road area, always willing to open local fêtes and similar events if his filming commitments allowed. As a child actor he appeared on stage in *White Horse Inn*, and was making movies before he was sixteen. Although he turned his talents to radio and television in the years before his untimely death, it is unlikely he will be forgotten as a film actor as long as there are repeats of *The Blue Lamp*, (in which he played the rookie constable) or *Henry V* (the Harfleur battle scenes).

The Plough inn, Beddington. The Plough stands on its own island at the northern end of Plough Lane, its name a reminder of the far-off days when the land grew some of the finest wheat in the county and Manor Farm and New Barn Farm kept local men in work. All that was to change with the outbreak of war in 1914 and the building of Beddington airfield, when more than 400 acres were requisitioned.

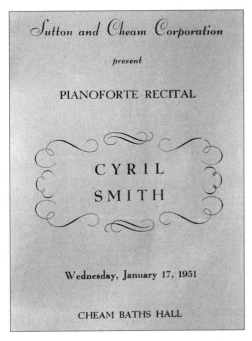

Cheam Baths Hall, Malden Road. The borough's new baths had opened in 1938, but it was not until after the Second World War that orchestral concerts, recitals, receptions and other events became a regular feature during the non-swimming season, when the pool was floored over. Mr Cyril Smith (below), the distinguished pianist, played several times at the baths hall, to capacity audiences. During the war he came to Nonsuch school and played for us; we all rushed out to buy his records after he had gone! Many years later I had the opportunity to go behind the scenes at the Royal Albert Hall, to thank him for introducing me to classical music.

Celebrating the coronation. Sutton's mayor and mayoress, Alderman and Mrs Kingsley Williams, led citizens in a full programme to mark the crowning of Her Majesty Queen Elizabeth II. Sporting events included cricket, athletics, boxing, swimming, gymnastics and bowls. There were several performances of Shakespeare's *Henry the Fifth*, a Flower, Fur and Feather show, carnival processions and a firework display that included 'a dazzling screen of aerial coruscations'. The celebrations culminated in an open-air religious service and rally at the borough stadium on the evening of Sunday 7 June 1953.

The Borough's Coronation Mayor and Mayoress

Alderman Kingsley Williams, J.P.   Mrs. Kingsley Williams

2 Park Cottages, Cheam, 1953. These weatherboarded cottages are similar to others in Park Road, Malden Road and Park Lane, possibly all erected at about the same time for Nonsuch estate workers. When coronation fever ran high and householders vied with each other to decorate everywhere red, white and blue, the window-boxes and flower-tubs of the cottages were a riot of patriotic colour.

Street party, June 1953. All the children in Belmont Road, Cross Road and Kings Road, Belmont, came in their fancy dress costumes to celebrate the Queen's coronation.

Golden wedding anniversary. My grandparents celebrated their anniversary with a family party, the centrepiece being the cake baked by Grannie and decorated by Gramp, who was a master baker and confectioner. He never got over the fact that the photographer would not give him time to put on a tie!

Carshalton Ponds, postwar. The ponds themselves are little changed, but pollution of different kinds is spoiling them. Bottles and other rubbish are thrown in, and the volume of traffic giving off noise and fumes is ruining what was once a lovely little corner of our world.

Beddington Park, 1950s. The River Wandle meanders across the park, in which stands Carew Manor (p. 21). The Grange is in the south-east of this area of parkland given over to leisure and sporting activities. In one place the river widens into a lake large enough for boating. The Wandle remains above ground as far as Purley Way, where Waddon ponds are our last reminder of a once vital source of power in the heyday of the mills.

Shinners, High Street, Sutton.† Popular radio and recording star, singer Alma Cogan – 'the girl with the giggle in her voice' – made a personal appearance in March 1956 at the opening of the new radio and record department of Shinners. Announcing the venture, Shinners said it was hoped the department would soon be able to give record recitals to customers in the restaurant.

Cheam Fair, 1955.† Tradition has it that the fair was first held in the thirteenth century by permission of the King, taking place each 15 and 16 May, though since 1680 it has been held on the 15th only. If no stall-holders appear on the appointed day, the village's right to have the fair will be lost forever. In 1951, Festival of Britain year, the local Ratepayers' Association tried to revive interest in the event; two years later, our Queen's coronation was seized on to promote the fair, with a programme that included 'the crowning of the Queen of the Fair'. Though the majority of these children look happy, there were rumblings among the grown-ups about the wet weather, the lack of support, and the doubts still cast on the validity of the whole thing.

Building Furzedown Road. One of Belmont's newer roads, Furzedown was created on land once part of the Bawtree family's home, Clapham Lodge. It links Downs Road in a double-S curve with Banstead Road South, emerging almost opposite Pine Walk. Comfortable houses with good-sized gardens in a then quiet district of near-countryside made this a most attractive residential area.

The Pirates of Penzance, April 1956. This photograph of the Parish of Cheam Amateur Operatic Society's production in the Parochial Rooms, gives a rare chance to see the interior of the old hall which has been used for so many purposes in its long history. From socials to flower shows, polling station to club meetings, its venerable walls have seen them all.

St Cecilia's Catholic Church, Stonecot Hill.†
During the Second World War it was agreed that the Catholic community in North Cheam was in need of its own church, and fundraising events began. Not until a decade after peace came was the step taken, when the Roman Catholic Bishop of Southwark, the Rt Revd Cyril C. Cowderoy (right of picture) laid the foundation stone. A sign of the times: in granting planning approval, Sutton and Cheam Council stipulated that there must be parking space in the church grounds for twenty cars.

AFTER AUSTERITY

The Gondoliers.† The combined talents
of singers from Sutton Grammar School
for Boys and Sutton High School for
Girls were on stage at the Public Hall
for several performances of this Gilbert
and Sullivan favourite during 1956.
A decade earlier, musicians from the
boys' school and Nonsuch girls had
combined to form an orchestra which
rehearsed at Cheam Common Junior
school (former Prime Minister John
Major's first school); students from
Sutton boys and Nonsuch sang excerpts
from Edward German's *Merrie England*
at Cheam. The only singers I remember
now are Joan Gater as Queen Elizabeth
and John Peckham (my neighbour in
Pelton Avenue) as Sir Walter Raleigh. He
sported a briar pipe, which he several
times let fall to the stage with a mighty
clatter.

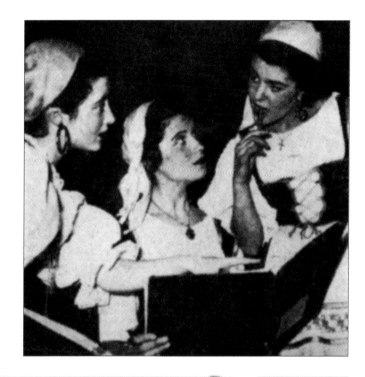

The Centre Court, Sutton Hard Courts.† Sutton's open tennis tournament was a regular event, attracting top names in the
run-up to Wimbledon. Players of the calibre for Davis and Wightman Cup events appeared, and others from Australia and
the United States would travel over to take part. One-thousand capacity crowds watched the 1956 finals.

The view from Hallmead Road, 1950s. Looking north (above), the main road leads to the famous Angel bridge, spanning the cutting made in the hill in Regency times (p. 40). Behind the trees on the right is All Saints church, Benhilton, and its burial ground. Looking south (below) towards Sutton town centre, the Cricketers inn is partly hidden by the trees on the left. Those on the right, with a police emergency telephone box at the path edge, obscure the site of the commemorative fountain (p. 27).

It's good to see so many old friends at my new shop!
56 High Street, Sutton

Old friends and new friends . . . you've been making it a real house-warming in the new Barratt's at 56, High Street, Sutton. I was here before, you remember, and then I left for some months, to let the builders in. Now it's a brand new shop, and I'm very proud of it.

As you know, I sell good shoes, fine-fashion shoes. But I sell comfort at the same time . . . two feet of comfort in every pair of shoes. Come and see my new premises, and all my new styles. Come and buy comfort *in* comfort! Welcome to my newest shop!

Walk the Barratt way
56-58 High Street, Sutton

'Walk the Barratt way.'† This long-established family firm of shoe manufacturers, based in Northampton, with its 'Mr Barratt' logo, had a branch at 56 High Street, Sutton, for some years. In 1956 they developed the site into a modern four-storey building (below), with floors above their retail shop for their display department. This comprised design studios, screen-printing and spray booths, a carpenter's shop, packaging room, draughtsmen's benches, and an empty office for the department's secretary, which she could have fitted out as she wished (see also p. 116).

Belmont Methodist Church, 1950s. The first church built was a 'tin tabernacle' known as The Mission, in Downs Road (1879). Small boys delighted in disturbing services by clattering pebbles onto the metal roof. Deterioration of the building after nearly forty years coincided with an increase in population 'over the bridge' (Station Road) and on 24 July 1915 (one year after that of St John's parish church), the foundation stone of a new building (the Free Church) on the corner of Kings Road was laid. In 1928 it was designated United Methodist (later Methodist) but demolished in the 1980s and replaced by Deacon Court. The Methodist Wesley Rooms in the parish church were dedicated in January 1988.

Miss Kelly meets her match, June 1956.†
A small boy named Tommy ruined the carefully laid plans of the matron and staff at St Mary's Children's Home, Sandy Lane, Cheam. Star guest actress Barbara Kelly came along to unveil a commemorative plaque above a cot, and Tommy was meant to sit in said cot, but it was nowhere near his bed-time, and he protested loudly. Even assurances from his favourite nurse that it was 'only pretend' could not pacify him.

Cheam war memorial. The memorial has continued to be a place to recall those who died in not only two world wars, but many other conflicts. A bugler sounds the Last Post (above) as civic leaders and members of the local community, headed by Sutton's mayor, Alderman D.P. Williams, prepare to observe the traditional two minutes' silence. Looking south-west from the lych-gate (below), the building in the centre background has been for very many years a printer's shop though once, I believe, it served as the village post office. To the right, the smallest cottage once had a boot and shoe repair shop downstairs; I think the Calcutt brothers worked there. In one of the larger buildings lived an elderly lady who, my mother often told me as we walked by, lost a son in the R101 air-ship disaster in France, in October 1930. All the cottages date from Tudor times, and are built in the same timber-framed and weather boarded style as the big house, Whitehall.

Sutton for the Cup. In 1963, Sutton United's football team, captained by Dave Hermitage (right) reached the final of the Amateur Cup and met Wimbledon (captain Roy Law, left) at Wembley. The referee was Mr K. Dagnall of Lancashire. From two-nil down, United fought back to draw level but, eight minutes from time, Wimbledon drew ahead again and 'almost on the whistle' the Dons made it four-two: so near yet so far. Note Sutton's coat of arms on Dave's shirt badge.

Sixties skyline. This was the time, before the introduction of tower blocks, when the only unwelcome intrusions on the skyline were these water-coolers, the power-station chimneys and the gasometer. Until the Second World War, the 'salt- and pepper-pot' towers of Crystal Palace could scarcely be ignored.

Views from the bridge. These photographs were taken in the 1960s by my cousin, from Belmont station bridge. Above is the scene looking west into Station Road with the parish church at the far end. Many of the shops remain in the same line of business, though the proprietors have changed. W. Taylor's premises are on the site of Huggett's (p. 49). Below, looking north towards Sutton, among the trees to the right are the 'prefabs' of Shanklin Road, put up as temporary homes, to ease the housing shortage after the Second World War, on land between the railway line and Brighton Road. The station itself is – not altogether the result of enemy bombing in 1940 – in a sorry state; the line was subsequently singled for the first time in 117 years of service to the village. Distant tower blocks give notice of the skyline of the future.

The old cottage, Cheam Broadway, 1960s. When road widening was considered around the village crossroads, the cottage was one of the major obstacles. It had been dated to about 1500 with a later lean-to extension, and was sufficiently prized by the community to warrant dismantling and rebuilding on its present site in 1922. Some of the timbers were then found to be even older than Tudor, suggesting that they were recycled from Cuddington, the village demolished by King Henry VIII to make way for Nonsuch Palace. The Onyx Property Investment Company, in developing this part of the Broadway, used a mock Tudor style, possibly to reflect the history of the area. To the right is the tall shop built in 1931 for Sainsbury.

Extension to Belmont parish church, 1966. The First World War had called a halt to the completion of the church, leaving a blank east wall and no tower for more than fifty years. The congregation chose the occasion of their Golden Jubilee to launch an appeal for £15,000 and four-year-old Jeremy Withers Green, with the help of his father Vicar Revd Timothy Withers Green (right) and Archdeacon W.S. Hayman (left) turned the first sod at the site of the west extension. It was to include a meeting-room with kitchen and cloakrooms above which was a nineteenth-century stained glass window – a gift from a demolished church at St Leonards, East Sussex.

Hill Road, 1960s. Not for much longer would the Public Hall and adjoining shops stand on the north corner of St Nicholas Road. Though still in use, their days were numbered: the hall was demolished in 1981, 103 years after it was built for £4,000. A number of well-known stage and radio actors made early appearances at the hall, including Jack Warner, Leslie Howard and Gladys Young.

Browns, 24 Station Road, Belmont, 1969. During the Second World War additional part-time staff had been engaged to release proprietor Harold Heyes (left) for service with the local NFS (National Fire Service), whose headquarters was almost next door to his shop. In the doorway stands Nigel Taylor. On his retirement in 1976, after fifty years at Browns, Harold was honoured with a presentation party at the local Constitutional Club by Belmont Traders Assocation.

Tom Burke, the Lancashire Caruso. After a colourful life in the opera houses of the world, Tom Burke, the ex-miner with the stirring tenor voice, chose to retire to Sutton. He moved into a house in Mayfield Road in 1965, speaking of plans to make the town into an opera centre. He is buried in Bandon Hill cemetery.

From Benhilton church, 1960s. Aimed to the south, my cousin's camera recorded the great changes to the skyline that had occurred in our lifetime. Once the tower of Trinity church (centre, far distance) was the only thing to thrust above the horizon, with the green of Surrey countryside beyond. Now, the first of the high-rises and mighty office blocks had put in an appearance.

Onward and Upward

Route 280: Tooting to Belmont, 1975. Buses on this route were earlier numbered 80 (going through to Kingswood), with 88 on Sundays. From Morden the 164 route also called at Belmont and went on to Banstead. Both routes called at the Sutton station bus stop, so Belmont passengers were very well served. The terminus at Belmont station was a turn-round area at the bottom of Downs Road, alongside a small café run by the Williams family, where drivers and conductors took refreshment breaks. Families coming to Belmont from London for 'a day in the country' were a source of amusement to local residents: the visitors alighted from the buses and set up their picnics on the nearest edge of the Downs, ignoring the wide open spaces beyond.

Nonsuch High School for Girls, 1981. Miss Marion McConnell Dickie MA, first headmistress of the school, celebrated her eightieth birthday by returning to Nonsuch for a party with over three hundred former pupils and staff. Here she is, seated second left, directing operations as of yore. The school had been open for only 16 months when the Second World War broke out, and for the next six years she shouldered responsibilties she could never have dreamed of when she became headmistress at the age of thirty-seven.

St Alban's Church, Cheam. In 1989/90, the church celebrated the diamond anniversary of its foundation. When, in 1929, it had been decided that the Gander Green Lane end of Cheam parish needed a church of its own, the rector and churchwardens were able to purchase beams, panelling, bricks and other materials from the demolished Cheam Court Farm, once one of the farms of Nonsuch Palace. The rambling ivy-covered farm house, parts of it 400 years old, had stood on the south-west corner of Cheam village crossroads, with a complex of barns, cow-sheds and out-houses. St Alban's was erected by Cheam builders Stevenson and Glyde, and became known as the Barn Church.

Park Cottages, Ewell Road, Cheam, 1990. Believed to have been built for workers on the Nonsuch estate (the park gates are across the road), before modernisation these small cosy houses retained many features of earlier days. The front door opened directly into the only living-room, from which two lift-the-latch doors led respectively to the kitchen (updated with half-size bath) and to the steep stairway, at the head of which were two box-like bedrooms with sloping floors and sounds of birds scurrying about in the roof-space. All doorways were low and wide, with wooden steps worn wafer-thin in the middle.

Robin Hood Lane, looking north, 1990s. The south end of this road (p. 18) was re-routed at the time St Nicholas Way was created, but it still led to the Robin Hood inn, little altered in appearance since Victorian times. The turning to the right in front of the inn is West Street, no longer running through to the High Street but ending at the ring road. West Street school closed in 1968 and was demolished five years later.

Nonsuch quadrangle, Jubilee celebrations 1987. The writer is with two of the earliest members of staff, Miss Callender (left) who taught her geography, and Miss Kenworthy (right) from whom she learned Latin. Miss Kenworthy was also form mistress to twenty-four overawed ten-year-olds who assembled as 'Form Lower One' in December 1939. The start of term had been delayed while air-raid shelters were dug in the grounds.

An old friend. The former Gwen Hayter of Belmont (front) was also at the reunion. During the Second World War, Gwen's father kept the Station Road grocer's shop next door to Browns (p. 107). In spite of food shortages and the extra rationing procedures he was required to attend to – registering customers, marking or clipping ration books, weighing out small amounts of food – Mr Hayter always seemed cheerful and welcoming when I went shopping there with Mother.

Penelope Keith. Actress Penelope Keith was born in Sutton and educated at Annecy Convent, Seaford, East Sussex, before attending the Webber Douglas dramatic school, making her first professional appearance in 1959. She was created many popular roles on stage, television and in movies, my own favourite being her disdainful hospital receptionist in an episode of the TV series *Two's Company* with Donald Sinden and Elaine Stritch. She now directs plays as well as starring in them, and for the year 2000 has narrated the ITN video of Her Majesty the Queen Mother's *One Hundred Glorious Years*.

Whitehall, Cheam, 1978. While we can only read about many of Cheam's old buildings Whitehall, once known as The Council House, is still with us, restored and cherished by a band of enthusiasts. The legend persists that Queen Elizabeth I, on one of her hunting trips to Nonsuch, chose this nearby yeoman farmer's home as the venue for an emergency meeting with her advisers. For almost 200 years, until purchased by Sutton and Cheam Borough Council in 1963, the house belonged to descendants of the Killick family. Major work was done in 1966 and 1975, with on-going research and restoration. Since 1978 the house has been open to the public, with a varied programme of events on offer.

Building the Holiday Inn, 1994. Redevelopment of the Cheam Road/Robin Hood Lane/Sutton Park Road area led to some bewildering changes in the landscape. The Inn, Central Library, School of Art and other civic buildings now stand where once were family homes and leafy lanes. The Secombe Theatre (p. 118) is off to the left of the photograph.

Nonsuch Old Girls' meeting, 1993. The writer was a Nonsuch pupil 1939–46, and featured a number of school pictures in *Cheam and Belmont in Old Photographs*, published in 1993. Former schoolmates invited her to an evening of reminiscences, also attended by several retired teachers including (centre) Miss Wood (mathematics).

Millennium

Produce stall, Sutton High Street, 2000. Far left was once the mouth of West Street, now closed off with part of the St Nicholas complex. Top Shop, behind it, was built in the 1930s for Perring's the furniture shop and replaced Fraser's opposite the Greyhound inn. One of the first high-rises was erected for Eagle Star Insurance. Pedestrianising a once noisy, traffic-blocked High Street and planting new trees have created an acceptable atmosphere for the new century.

Barratts, 176 High Street, Sutton. After some years at no. 56 (p. 101), Barratts moved from their four-storey building and for a while this long-established shoe firm's only outlet in Sutton was within another fashion store. In about 1995, however, a new shop opened at no. 176 in the pedestrians' part of the High Street. This is one of the properties whose façade above street level has changed very little in many years.

Sutton High Street, 2000. Gradually the old terraces that lined the street have disappeared, first with updating of shop-fronts, then complete demolition. Below Throwley Road, in the upper part of the east side today, only a couple of shops retain the original upper storeys, with mouldings and other trimmings still featured. To the right is the store, now occupied by Wilkinson's, that replaced the Municipal Offices (p. 25) in 1970. Behind the gables of nos 84 and 86 looms the massive Surrey House in Throwley Way.

The former Arcade, 2000. Although the original arch at the eastern end has survived (below), gone are Mr Shinner's high glass roof and all the little shops (p 67)

The Secombe Theatre, Cheam Road, 2000. The former Christian Science church was converted into the Secombe Centre in 1982, run by a trust, with a Council grant. It was formally opened on 16 January 1983 by Sir Harry Secombe MBE (p. 89). Four years later, the local authority itself took over the administration, transferred to the London Borough of Sutton in 1965 and, after refurbishment which included increasing the seating capacity to 406, re-named it the Secombe Theatre, with Sir Harry as patron. The design for the exterior statue of a figure wearing the masks of Comedy and Tragedy was the winner of a competition for aspiring artists.

The Red Lion, Park Road, Cheam, 2000. On Cheam Fair Day, 15 May, the garden stall on the pub forecourt was doing a good trade. The Red Lion, justifiably called 'Ye Olde', has stood on this site, externally little altered, for at least four hundred years. Long ago, vestry meetings dealing with local administration were held twice a year at the inn, which once upon a time gave its name to the road.

Cheam Fair, 2000. The fair has survived for more than five hundred years, though occasionally it has hung on by the skin of its teeth. One year during the Second World War my father came home with the news that a solitary man was standing in Park Road with a tray of small home-made items, thus establishing that the fair had been held and so must be allowed to continue in future times. In millennium year, 15 May fell on a weekday and mainly local groups such as Cheam Women's Institute (left) and Elisa Dongworth, Chairman of the Friends of Cheam Library (above) set up tables. When it falls on a Saturday and the children are out of school, it has much more of a fairground atmosphere.

Pearson's bicycle shop, 2000. I was delighted, when researching for this book, to find the business still in family hands, with Pearson brothers William (left) and Guy (right). That part of the dear old High Street may now be dubbed Times Square – and pedestrianised at that – but the tradition of dealing in cycles and accessories goes on. What old Mr Pearson's Edwardian customers would have thought of today's town centre cycle races, to say nothing of the brief clothes now worn, does not bear thinking about.

St Nicholas parish church, 2000. One thousand local children were each given a leaf-shaped card and asked to write on it their hopes for the new millennium. Hung on the branches of this metal tree, designed by local art students, and placed in the Lady Chapel in sight of worshippers and visitors to the church, their simple messages convey a wealth of trust and optimism to older generations.

Acknowledgements

This book is based on a lifelong collection of anecdotes, souvenirs, family albums and photographs which at a distance of time have needed to be researched and checked. This I have done by referring to a variety of books and pamphlets, but have not knowingly infringed any copyright. I gladly acknowledge the help and advice of the following: Brenda, Bob and Bill (St Dunstan's, Cheam), Christine (Barratts), Barbara Edser (Cheam), John Goodman and Stan Fullerton (Seaford Museum), Mr Hiarns (Worcester Park Royal British Legion), Sue James (Sutton High School), Valerie Pinborough (Wallington Girls' School), Shirley, Valerie and Samantha (Secombe Theatre), staff at All Saints Parish Church, Sutton, Mr George Hoole, William and Guy Pearson, Professor John White, Mrs Lillian Tertis, Mr Kahn of Khan & Averill (publishers), Revd Edward Probert, London Management for Miss Penelope Keith, Mrs Maggie Hanley. Special appreciation for the photographs and reminiscences contributed to this book by my cousin Kenneth, who did not live to see it published.

Photographs marked * appear by courtesy of Sutton Heritage Centre, and those marked † are reproduced by kind permission of the Croydon Advertiser Group. Very special thanks go to Simon Fletcher, Fiona Eadie and Annabel Fearnley of Sutton Publishing for guidance and advice, and to Barry, Freda and Nigel of Seaford Fotobox for their unfailing patience with my photography.

Except as indicated, none of the pictures reproduced appears to be under copyright, but the current practice of marketing photographic copies means the original details on their backs are not available. Apologies are rendered for any source not fully cleared or acknowledged; a note to the publishers in such case will ensure an amendment in any reprint.

Old photographs such as those found in antique shops or at postcard fairs seldom identify the people depicted; I apologise for any distress caused to their descendants, and invite them to contact me through the publishers if they would like to claim such photographs.